Wolfgang Amadeus MOZART

Mass in C

K. 317

"Coronation"

(Otto Taubmann)

Vocal Score
Klavierauszug

SERENISSIMA MUSIC, INC.

CONTENTS

1. Kyrie 3

2. Gloria 7

3. Credo 20

4. Sanctus 38

5. Benedictus 42

6. Agnus Dei 48

ORCHESTRA

2 Oboes, 2 Bassoons
2 Horns, 2 Trumpets, 3 Trombones, Timpani
Organ
Violin I, Violin II, Violoncello, Double Bass

Duration: ca. 30 minutes
First performance: Easter Sunday, April 4, 1779
Salzburg Cathedral
Soli, Chorus and Orchestra with the composer directing

Complete orchestral parts compatible with this vocal score are available (Cat. No. A2694) from
E. F. Kalmus & Co., Inc.
6403 West Rogers Circle
Boca Raton, FL 33487 USA
(800) 434 - 6340
www.kalmus-music.com

Mass in C
K. 317
1. Kyrie

W. A. Mozart
Piano reduction by Otto Taubmann
Edited by Karel Torvik

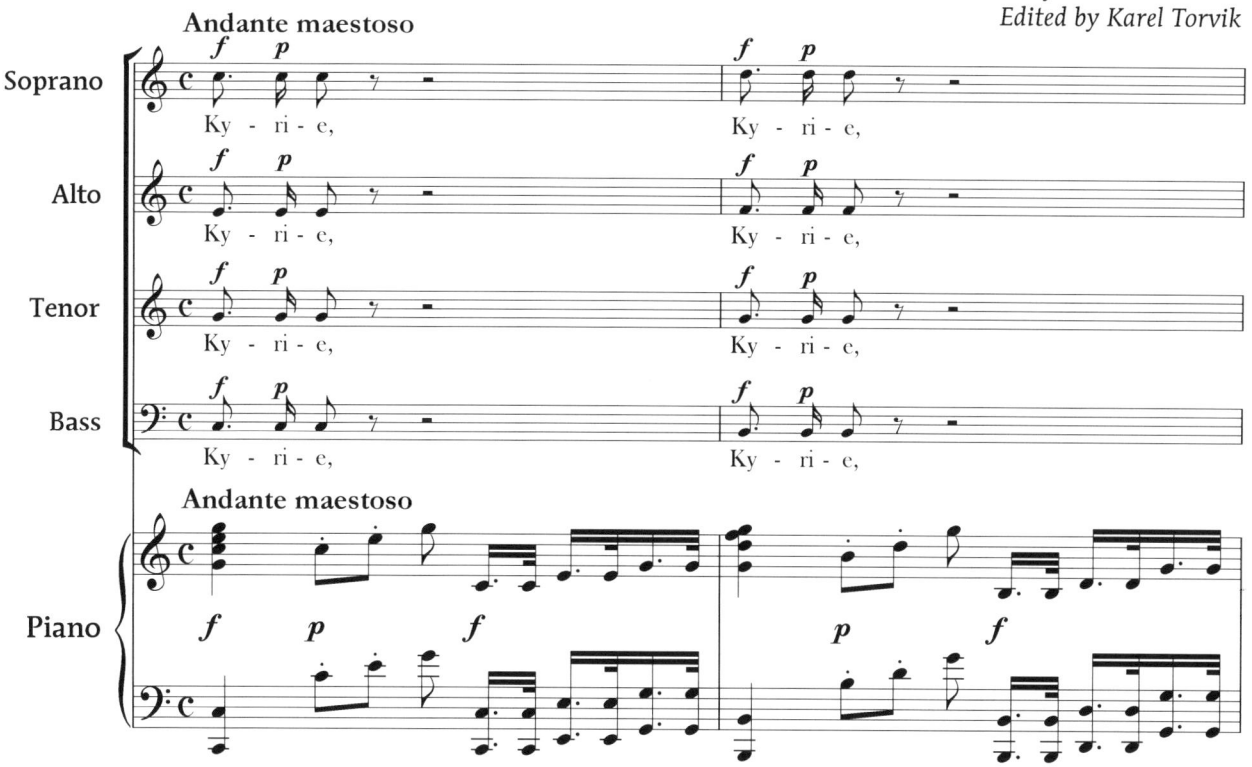

© Copyright 2007 Serenissima Music, Inc.
All rights reserved. Printed in USA

2. Gloria

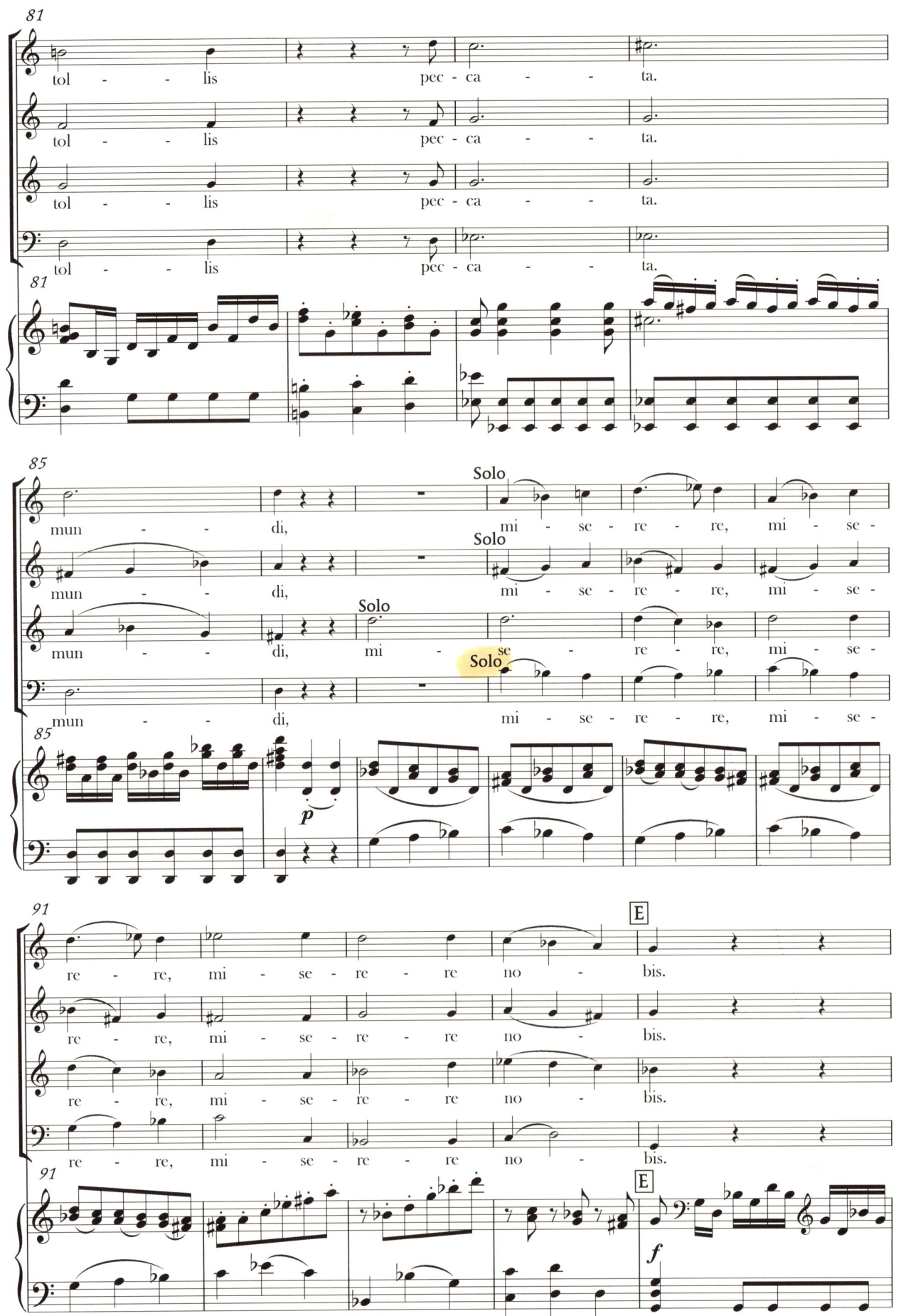

3. Credo

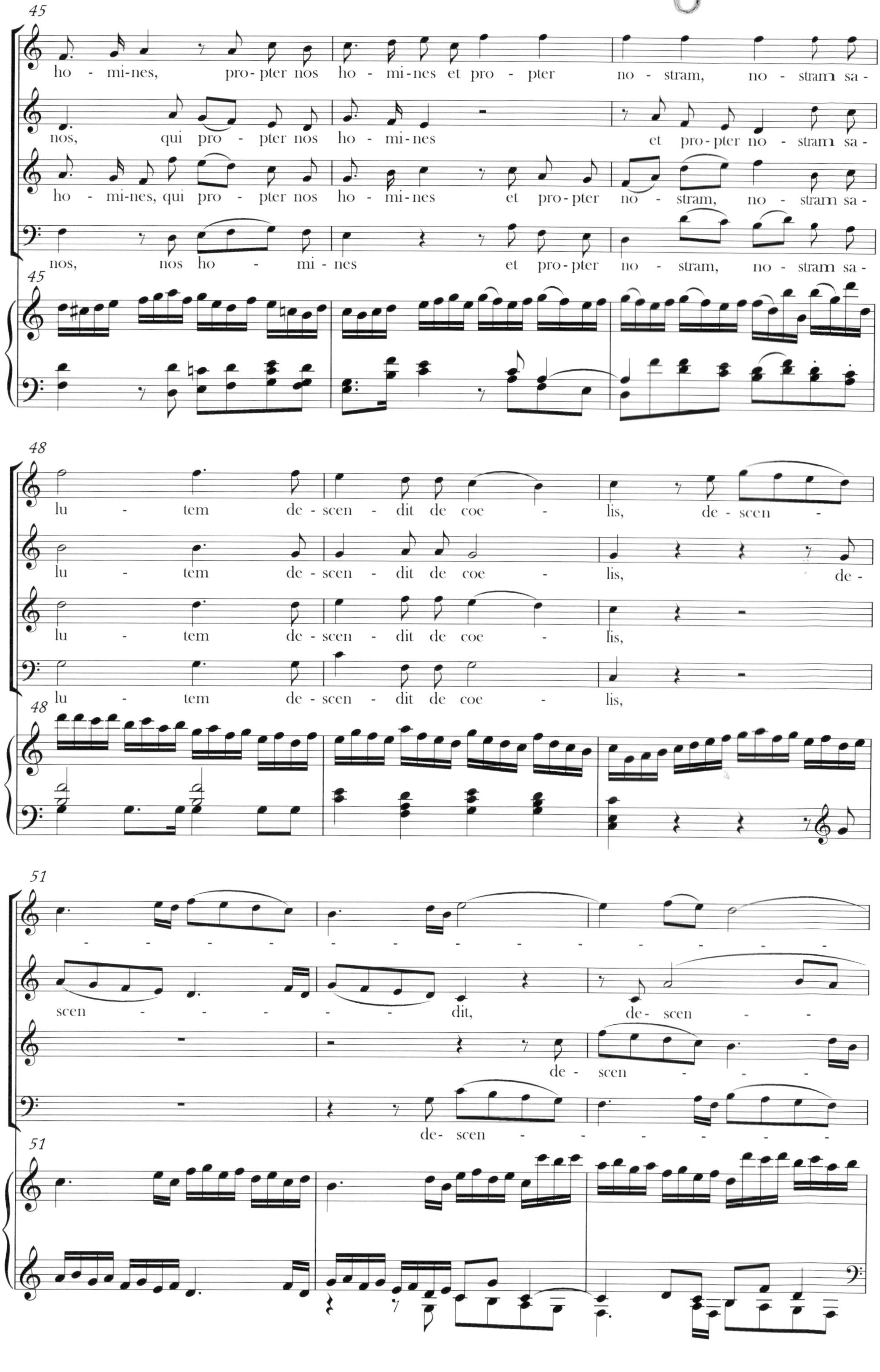
45
ho - mi-nes, propter nos ho - mi-nes et pro - pter no - stram, no - stram sa -
nos, qui pro - pter nos ho - mi-nes et pro-pter no - stram sa -
ho - mi-nes, qui pro - pter nos ho - mi-nes et pro-pter no - stram, no - stram sa -
nos, nos ho - mi - nes et pro-pter no - stram, no - stram sa -
48
lu - tem de - scen - dit de coe - lis, de - scen -
lu - tem de - scen - dit de coe - lis, de -
lu - tem de - scen - dit de coe - lis,
lu - tem de - scen - dit de coe - lis,
51
scen - dit, de - scen -
de - scen -
de - scen -

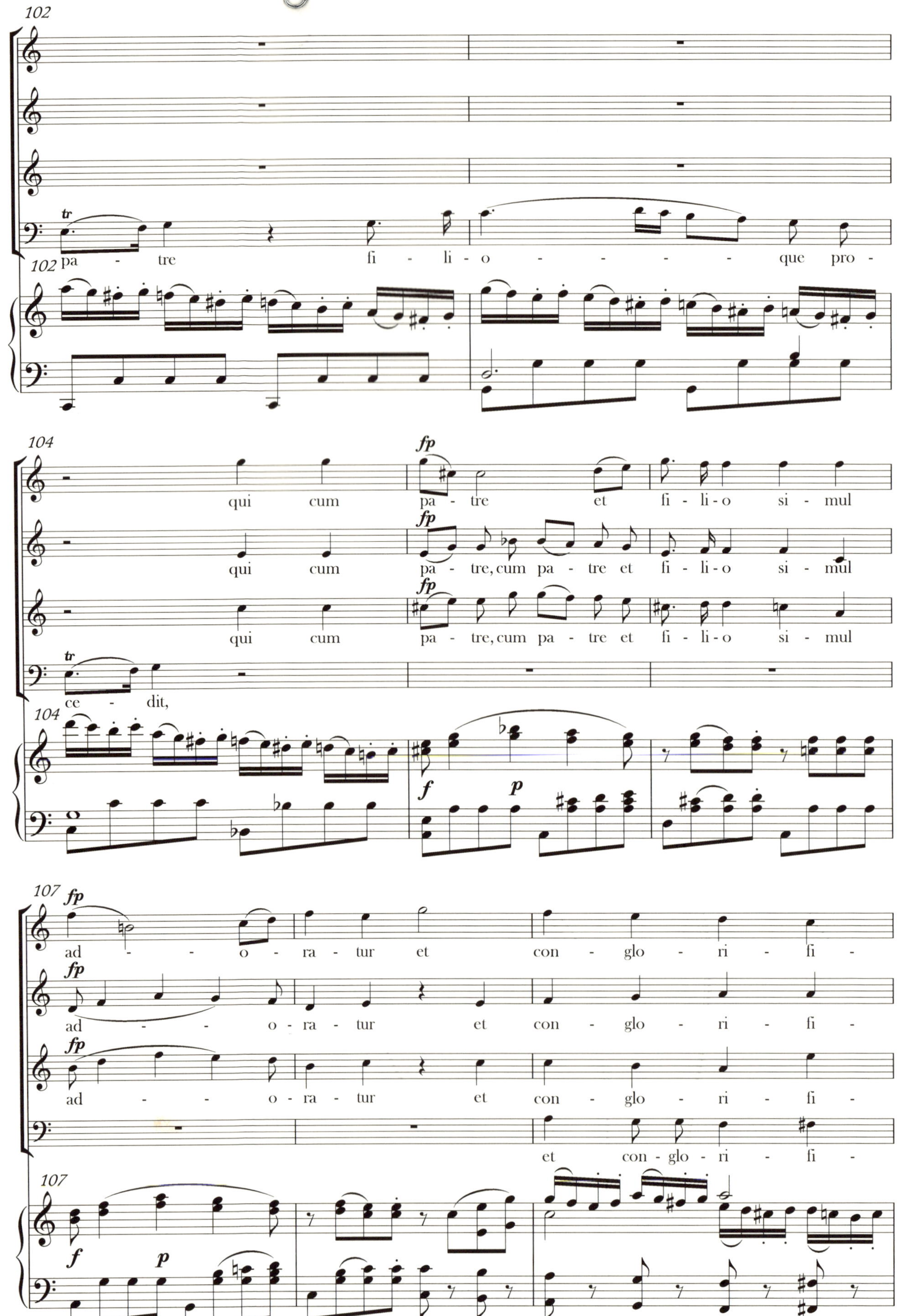
102
tr
pa - tre fi - li - o - - - - que pro -
104
qui cum pa - tre et fi - li - o si - mul
qui cum pa - tre, cum pa - tre et fi - li - o si - mul
qui cum pa - tre, cum pa - tre et fi - li - o si - mul
ce - dit,
fp
f p
107
ad - - o - ra - tur et con - glo - ri - fi -
ad - - - o - ra - tur et con - glo - ri - fi -
ad - - - o - ra - tur et con - glo - ri - fi -
et con - glo - ri - fi -

4. Sanctus

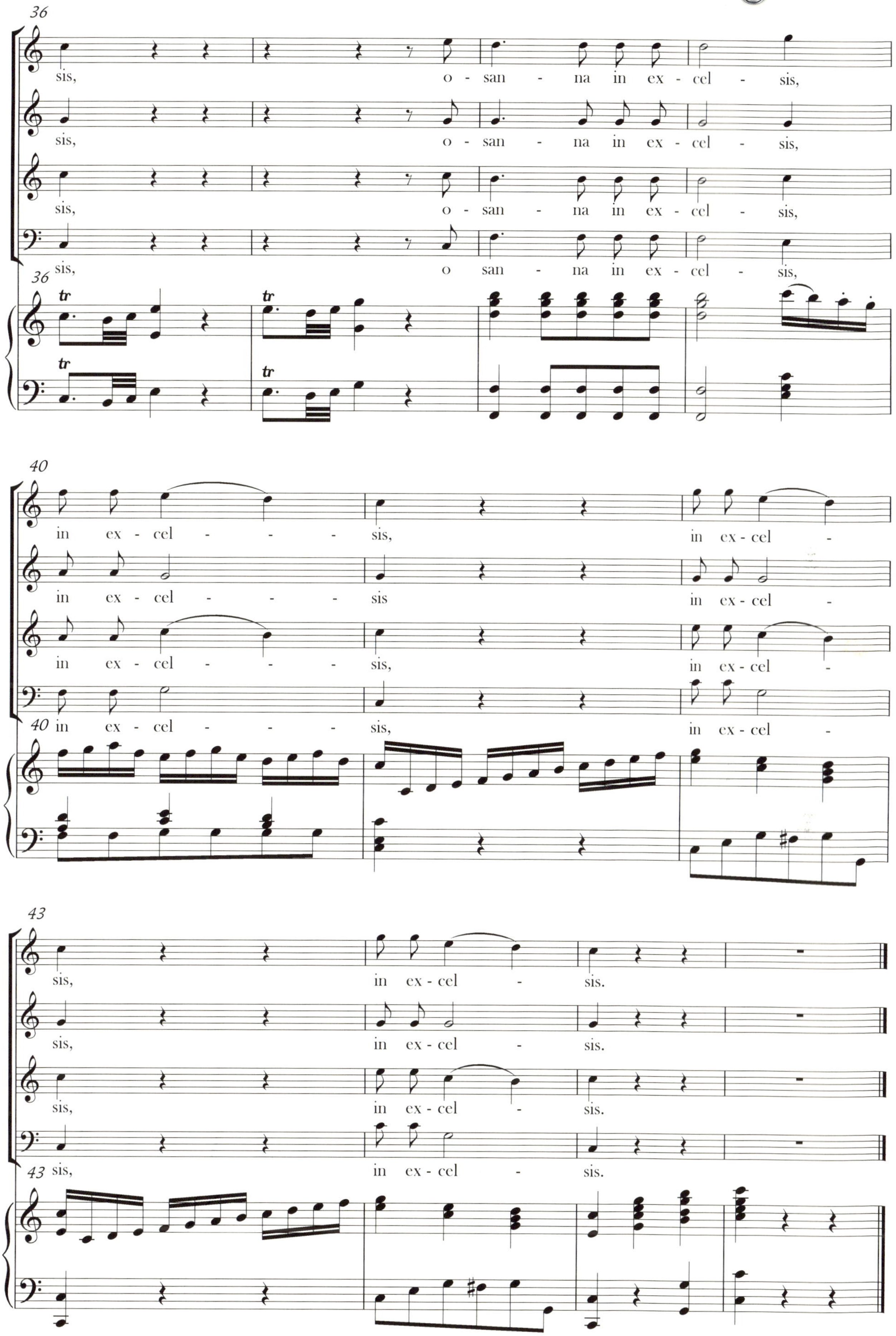
36
sis, o - san - na in ex - cel - sis,
sis, o - san - na in ex - cel - sis,
sis, o - san - na in ex - cel - sis,
sis, o san - na in ex - cel - sis,
36
tr
tr
tr
tr
40
in ex - cel - - - sis, in ex - cel -
in ex - cel - - - sis in ex - cel -
in ex - cel - - - sis, in ex - cel -
40 in ex - cel - - - sis, in ex - cel -
43
sis, in ex - cel - sis.
sis, in ex - cel - sis.
sis, in ex - cel - sis.
43 sis, in ex - cel - sis.

5. Benedictus

6. Agnus Dei

Made in the USA
Middletown, DE
26 March 2019